ISBN: 9781707108756

It is a captivating love that occurs
When it is love for self that one prefers
A stable self-esteem self-love stirs
When the first reflection she learns to love is hers

Pretty Simple

There is a beauty upon her face that cannot compare to her beauty within

When does she feel most pretty, well, that depends

Maybe it's when she snuggles next to her mother sipping hot cocoa while reading a book

Or riding the back of her father while displaying a cheery look

Playing games with siblings while laughing laughs that hurt the gut

Or looking into the mirror and loving who she sees minus ifs, ands or buts

Could it be the lazy days that don't require much

Or unkempt hair with a face that makeup has never touched

Maybe it's all those things that cause her to love the makeup of her temple

One of many more that make feeling pretty, pretty simple

"PRETTY IS YOUR BEAUTY INSIDE AND OUT...THE INSIDE OF YOU IS BEING REFLECTED ONTO YOUR OUTSIDE"

ASHLIE, 17

What do you love about yourself?

MOMENTS IN THE MIRROR

I will look in the mirror and love who I see

I will embrace my collection of flaws as signs that celebrate my individuality

Pretty Filtered

In a world of likes and follows, and pretty that's vainly shallow
It has become increasingly difficult to know
Which version of me to be when the likes don't proceed when the real me I show
Did she care to ask how the filtered mask presented a different her
Or that the likes and follows are empty and hallow or maybe it did not occur
The best of you is flawed and imperfect and are gifts that none can share
Worthy of being shown unfiltered as it was God who placed them there
The best of you, all beautifully true, is yours to own alone
And no amount of foundation can cover the pretty that God placed on
Your makeup is freckles and lips, kinky hair and long fingertips
Cheeks with dimples and faces with pimples
Feet big or small and heights short or tall
Pretty, in its vast forms, armors you with protection
Permitting you to be perfectly true to the honesty of your reflection
A stern rejection to the opinions and judgments found in other's projections
Because your election is to learn to be the object of your own affection

"PRETTY IS ME! IT'S WHATEVER APPEALS TO YOU AND WHAT SPEAKS TO YOUR SOUL AND SPIRIT."

SABRINA, 50

WHY IS IT IMPORTANT FOR YOU TO GENUINELY LIKE YOURSELF?

I will look in the mirror and love the person staring back at me

I will acknowledge her reflection of worthiness that God himself placed within me

Pretty Comprehended

You are the work of the Creator's hands molded as he intended

And loving yourself as you are is the prettiest when you comprehend it

"PRETTY IS BEING NATURAL AND FULLY COMFORTABLE IN YOUR OWN SKIN. PRETTY IS CONFIDENCE!"

ANGELA, 38

LIST THREE PEOPLE WHO YOU VIEW AS PRETTY, INSIDE AND OUT, AND WHY.

NAME: ______________________________

____

____

____

NAME: ______________________________

____

____

____

NAME: ______________________________

____

____

____

I will look in the mirror and not compare another to me
Because God allows her to be pretty without taking
any from me

Pretty Wonderful

Fearfully and wonderfully made is how I came to be

Of the many ingredients it took, pretty was of high degree

Our Creator created us equipped with something special to display

A million forms of wonderful all intertwined in our DNA

Imagine God stating in Word that you are the head and not the tail

And even in your most trying times you were created to prevail

Imagine God knowing of your greatness while you rested in the womb

To live out your greatness is a praise as sweet to his nostrils as a delicate perfume

....and that praise does he consume

"I THINK PRETTY IS NOT WHAT IS OUTSIDE BUT INSIDE OF YOU. PRETTY IS SOMETHING THAT HAS NOTHING TO DO WITH OTHERS BUT ONLY HOW YOU FEEL ABOUT YOURSELF: LIKE, YOU SHOULD BE KIND, ENCOURAGING, SMART, LEARNING NEW THINGS...ALL THAT MAKES YOU PRETTY...TO ME."

ISREAL, 8

What makes you wonderful?

I will look in the mirror and I will smile

Because I love the skin I'm in and I'll be in it for quite a while

Pretty Inside

Inside first does pretty grow and to the outside does pretty shine

What is not pretty inwardly, pretty can only loosely define

It's easy to love others when love starts with my own towards me

It's easy to love myself when I believe I was made wonderfully

It's easy to believe I'm exceptional when I first believe in the power of the One who created the world

Because if he had enough pretty to paint the sky surely, he had some left for this little girl

"PRETTY IS MORE THAN YOUR OUTWARD BEAUTY. PRETTY IS THE TRUE YOU ON THE INSIDE...IT'S THE LOVE YOU GIVE, HOW YOU CARE, YOUR KIND SPIRIT. LETTING YOUR INNER BEAUTY OUTSHINE YOUR OUTER BEAUTY IS PRETTY TO ME."

CARMELITA, 38

WHEN DO YOU FEEL MOST PRETTY?

MOMENTS IN THE MIRROR

I look in the mirror and I feel no shame
Because God, knowing my flaws, chose to die for me
all the same

Pretty It Is

It was love at first sight that captivated her
A symphony of pretty that collided onto her
It is the mole placed intentionally upon the roof of her cheek
It is the sound of her own laugh and the squeak when she would speak
It is the gap between her front teeth and the wrinkles that rest upon her forehead when she smiles
It is the small scar alongside her elbow from a fall as a child
It is the depths of curious browns that penetrate her eyes
And salty tears that flow from them when she's angry or when she cries
It is the positioning of her ears and legs that slightly bow
It is the pigment of her skin intertwined with a toughness she is often too shy to show
It is the way she ponders her thoughts to ensure they don't offend
It is the way she stands her ground when those thoughts she must defend
It is the moments she understands her wrong and an apology she will give
It is the way she allows forgiveness to enhance the quality in which she lives
It is a smile when she looks into the mirror and a love for who it is she sees
It is an acceptance of self that makes loving herself a breeze

"PRETTY TO ME IS HOW I FEEL ON ANY PARTICULAR DAY. IT IS EVERCHANGING AND CONTROLLED BY MY EMOTIONS AND MOOD. PRETTY IS MY ATTITUDE, MY CONFIDENCE, MY WORTH, MY LAUGH, MY SMILE, EVEN WHAT I CONSIDER TO BE MY IMPERFECTIONS. PRETTY IS SIMPLY ME BEING WHO I AM!"

VALERIE, 38

A Note To Self: Create Your Own Affirmation

MOMENTS IN THE MIRROR

I look in the mirror and I see a perfect me

And yes, I get to define what's perfect about the perfect me I see

Pretty Learned

She saturates her daughter's learning with words that penetrate her growth

So, her daughter can absorb an understanding based upon the statutes of this oath

I promise to choose to be phenomenal in ways that I only can

To elevate my pretty to levels few can understand

To never allow words of others to shake my foundation

Instead be true to the words built upon my own self-revelation

I will love myself deeper and wider than anyone ever could

I will forgive myself quicker than only Jesus Christ would

I will stand tall in my greatness and let no one minimize

The pretty I love within with no compromise

The flawless Creator created a flawlessly me

And the flaws I gathered just add to my version of pretty

Lessons taught and lessons learned

Self-worth sought and self-worth earned

She is my mother and it is by the weight of her examples that teach me to be

The greatest form of pretty that she first birthed inside of me

"PRETTY IS BEING A LEADER AND NOT A FOLLOWER...JUST BEING YOURSELF...AND KNOWING THAT'S ENOUGH"

Zauryn, 10

WHO DOES GOD SAY I AM?

WRITE DOWN SCRIPTURES THAT DEFINE WHO YOU ARE.

I look in the mirror and this I've come to understand
There can be no flaws in a woman shaped by God's hands
If He said I was beautifully made then that has to be true
So there can be no flaws as He has made those beautiful too

Pretty Today

Dear yesterday, how I wish I loved the way I love today
To myself there's so much I neglected to say
But yesterday was yesterday
If I could tell her that God sees her more valuable than man could ever measure
That her heart, though fragile, is her most precious treasure
That she is stronger than she believes and more intelligent than she knows
That she will come to believe this the more she grows
That her tears of insecurity are from the eyes of a girl who will one day say
Those same eyes realize her pretty and she feels beautiful today

"PRETTY IS A COMBINATION OF SELF-LOVE, SELF-AWARENESS, AND SELF-CARE EXPRESSED OUTWARDLY THROUGH THE WAY YOU TAKE CARE OF YOURSELF, CARRY YOURSELF, AND GRACIOUSLY ACCEPT THE GOOD GIFTS THAT GOD PROVIDES TO YOU."

CANDISS, 45

LOOKING BACK, WHAT DO YOU WISH YOU WOULD HAVE APPRECIATED ABOUT YOURSELF SOONER?

MOMENT IN THE MIRROR

I look in the mirror and I will speak to myself
I will continuously say how much I love myself
That I am worthy of love and that love I must securely carry
Onto the next woman whose love for self tarried

Pretty Home

Built of stone yet delicate are her walls

That guard her heart in various forms of tall

Strong enough to protect yet weak enough to puncture

A pretty that molds the foundation of her infrastructure

Wide are the windows that expose the toughness of her heart

It's a messy yet beautiful form of art

Perched outside her attic nestled upon the roof of her mind

Adorning her with majesty as invisible as time

Is a crown that is her very own

Giving her contentment that feels like home

"MODERATELY BEAUTIFUL...YET DELICATE. NATURALLY ALLURING ON THE INSIDE AND OUT."

MELANIE, 39

Pretty Life

Somewhere back there, along the trail of her journey, she abandoned her self -love moving forward while it stayed behind
It trailed her for years hoping she would soon find it in time
Instead, she piled layers of life experiences upon its fragile neck
It stayed suffocating by the hands of hurt, brokenness and neglect
Her decisions buried it even further as pain in various forms she learned to collect
And its absence was evident in the choices she'd select

Though the world sees a surfaced smile, its root is an internal frown
As she learned how to be a queen that had abandoned her spiritual crown
A mask of pretty she perched upon her face so the world would never know
The depths of sorrows that plague her mind are truths she didn't want to show
Her tears were from the void that self-love could only fill
And though it was close and willing to occupy that space that loneliness filled
It had to be asked in, accepted at all cost
It would mean she would have to abandon the products of her own abandonment if she was ever to return from lost
It would mean she had to turn from accepting hurt from those that hurt
It means that she would have to accept failure piecing together a relationship that was never meant to work

With a man that knows only the worth that she knew
So he treated her as she accepted because that's all he knew to do
Despite her tries, she could never love him more than she was capable of loving herself
So, what she accepted was not a reflection of her love for him but a reflection of her lack of love for self.

Like many prodigals, her journey back to self came via lessons taught in lonesome lows
Her history brought her a shame only honest exposure controls
The longer she exposed the seed of her truth to the light the more she blossomed and matured
Because shame dies when it's not preserved by lies and regrets of what you endured
The beauty about brokenness is the way in which God shines when you are healed
To re-read the chapters in your story and see in the dead moments He lives
Who said that she wasn't as pretty in her low as she is in her high
Who said that she ever stopped being the apple of the Lord's eye
Who said that she was lost to a world lacking any resemblance of kind
Who said that she was unworthy of the self-love she would humbly find
Who said that journeys are easy, that tears wouldn't flow without measure from your eyes
Who said it doesn't hurt when, to the Lord, the old you dies
There are many forms of pretty but only one that would define her
And that is the pretty self-love gives the moment it was believed by her

PRETTY IS HUMILITY

SHE IS HUMBLE ENOUGH TO KNOW

THAT PRETTY IS JUST PRETTY UNLESS SHE HAS THE INTEGRITY TO SHOW

I AM SPECIAL
I AM FREE
I AM VICTORIOUS
I AM ME

Made in USA - Kendallville, IN
1185953_9781707108756
10.26.2020 1342